The Motorhome Story

The Motorhome Story

Andrew Jenkinson

The
History
Press

Andrew Jenkinson has had published twelve books on touring caravans, static caravans and motorhomes, and writes for Future Publications titles *Practical Caravan* and *Practical Motorhome*, as well as *Park Home Holiday Living* magazine. He also contributes to the Caravan and Motorhome Club and the Camping and Caravanning Club. He has appeared on both TV and radio and has an archive stretching back to the early 1920s. He also tests new/used tourers, motorhomes and holiday caravans and belongs to two large classic caravan clubs. He lives on the outskirts of Blackpool in Lancashire.

First published 2021

The History Press
97 St George's Place, Cheltenham,
Gloucestershire, GL50 3QB
www.thehistorypress.co.uk

British Library Cataloguing in Publication Data.
A catalogue record for this book is available from the British Library.

ISBN 978 0 7509 9490 3

Typesetting and origination by The History Press
Printed in Turkey by Imak

Contents

Foreword

The rise of the motorhome and campervan over the last fifteen plus years has been remarkable in the UK. However, in the rest of Europe, the motorhome has seen even more growth due to the increased amenities for users with plentiful stopovers and water points. Even so, the UK has seen motorhome and campervan sales climb higher each year. With a vast choice of brands, layouts and models, the motorhome is now a popular leisure vehicle.

This book looks at how the motorhome was first an idea for mobile holidaying in the early 1900s. Then known as a motorised caravan, the motorhome was ahead in the trailer versus motorhome stakes.

The motorhome is basically a caravan body attached to a chassis and cab, and was seen to be more mobile, but no manufacturer was producing such a vehicle. It was a rich man's leisure pursuit, so motorhomes were built to special order in the early part.

This book looks at the design of the motorhome and its accessories over time, as well as looking at where users went with their leisure vehicles from the early years to the present. This isn't a book of the A–Z of motorhome manufacturers; it's the general story of how the motorhome progressed from an eccentric rich person's idea to the lifestyle it is today. Even the 113-year-old Caravan Club felt compelled to change its title to the Caravan & Motorhome Club a few years ago, to keep up with growing trends.

This book concentrates, then, on the birth of the coach-built motorhome; how it began; and its status in the present day. Sit back and read how what was once a crude idea has become the sophisticated leisure vehicle of today.

Andrew Jenkinson

Most of the material featured in this book comes from my own vast archives. All images are from the author's collection unless otherwise stated; in the event of any omission, please contact me care of the publishers.

1.

The Foundation Stone is Laid

The early beginnings of the motorhome can be traced back to the early 1900s. Those early attempts at living quarters mounted on the back of a motorised chassis were primitive, as you would expect. With the appearance of the first automobiles, it became apparent that travel was restricted, mainly due to reliability problems, but also because the roads were not suitable for this new form of transport.

The roads drastically needed to be improved. The road system was particularly problematic in winter, with mud causing cars to get stuck. In rural areas, many roads were basically tracks.

However, as road building improved and macadam roads gradually replaced tracks, the early car owners (rich folk!) began to look to travel further afield.

Where most people would normally see little of the UK, the car opened up a new vista, which meant motoring holidays became a novel and growing trend. But, with the possibilities of a day's travel limited by time and road networks, this saw motorists turn to hotels as the answer. For the cyclist, the concept of camping was brought to the fore as a cheap, budget-friendly adventure break.

Dr Gordon Stables' Wanderer was the beginning of the modern leisure vehicle, both towed and self-propelled.

Caravanning for the leisure user began in the late 1800s and was pioneered by Dr Gordon Stables, with his horse-drawn caravan built specially for him, named the Wanderer. The idea of roaming the country without a care in the world appealed to the gentry, who wanted to be able to roam like the Gypsies – although they looked at it all through romantic eyes. In fact, they took servants and had specially designed horse-drawn caravans with the servants living outside.

The jottings of Dr Stables saw several books published, telling of his adventures. By 1907, a small club was founded by J. Harris Stone and named the Caravan Club. The new Caravan Club consisted of horse-drawn caravans, which were sometimes left on a pitch for several weeks before moving off.

Previous to this, another club had been formed – the Camping Club. With a more mobile public and the new safety bicycle, the less well-off could go cycling to a camping destination for a weekend or longer.

Soon, a small industry developed supplying tents, stoves and other camping equipment. An accessory market began to slowly evolve, with shops selling camping equipment. (Toilet tents were common back then and became an essential must-have!) This crossed over to the new caravan movement, which was gaining momentum.

As the 1900s progressed, the car was slowly becoming more common, although getting mobile to go on holiday was still a rich man's hobby. It was also becoming more reliable, and it now enabled the wealthy to go further afield and camp. Some owners would sleep in the car and cook outside with the tent. Some also tried to adapt their cars to offer accommodation. The few who did this were soon to find out that the extra weight affected both the handling of the vehicle and the power of the engine.

The idea of using a vehicle-pulled trailer as accommodation was also being used with steam-driven vehicles. This was utilised by the army, towing a large four-wheel trailer of supplies, which could also sleep soldiers in bunks.

*In 1907, the Caravan Club was formed for the horse-drawn
leisure caravan. Motorhomes did join but were not encouraged.*

One account of an early motorhome was in 1900 when a Daimler owner in the West Country converted his vehicle for sleeping. No images were available, but comments later described the attempt as a mere 'camping car' design.

THE
SAUCEPAN
BOILING SET

THE
KETTLE
BOILING SET

A few other accessories will be found listed on page 61

Equipment used for the early motorhome of the 1900s.

A toilet tent was essential for the first motorhome users!

In 1902, a Dr Lehwass constructed a crude motorhome (of sorts) from his Panhard Levassoor car. He was ambitious, because his idea was to tour the globe and, I presume, write about his adventures. A 25hp engine was to haul his motorhome, which apparently had a foldaway bed and even a stove – no doubt of a camping design.

He had raised great interest among inquisitive onlookers, who would cheer and wave him off from Hyde Park Corner, as the vehicle moved slowly into action. But although it was slow and no easy feat to drive, it made it to St Petersburg in Russia, where he unfortunately became snowed in.

The doctor abandoned the idea and his primitive design to the snows. However, some months later it was shipped back to the UK, although nothing was heard of it again!

Fun fact: The early motorhome trundling through a remote village often caused young children to run indoors in fright!

It would need a commercial set-up with money and innovative ideas to pursue the idea of a manufactured motorhome. One French company did produce a motorhome, naming it the Maison Automobile. The practical design was shown at the 1904 Société Nationale des Beaux-Arts exhibition. It caused interest but it wasn't commercially a success and became more of a one-off.

The leisure horse-drawn caravan was gaining popularity, with the Caravan Club having several meets in places such as the New Forest. Would the idea of a motorised vehicle with living accommodation take off at this early stage?

In the UK, the motorhome had already been seen as a potential new leisure idea by some with forward vision. A Mr J.B. Mallalieu, who lived in Wavertree, Liverpool, had in fact thought of building a motorhome in 1906 that would be more practical than some of the one-off ideas that had seen the light of day in this period. Using a chassis made by the Belsize Motor Co. of Manchester, it came with a 40hp engine.

Mr Mallalieu had the chassis delivered to a coachbuilder. Using his own ideas, he had possibly designed the first practical motorhome in the UK, built with what was described at the time as a 'long' 6m vehicle. It was also 2m wide, and the vehicle was said to weigh over 2,040kg (its 40hp engine would certainly struggle). It also cost over £1,000!

J. Harris Stone, the founder of the Caravan Club, with his horse-drawn caravan. Harris wasn't at first impressed with early motorhomes.

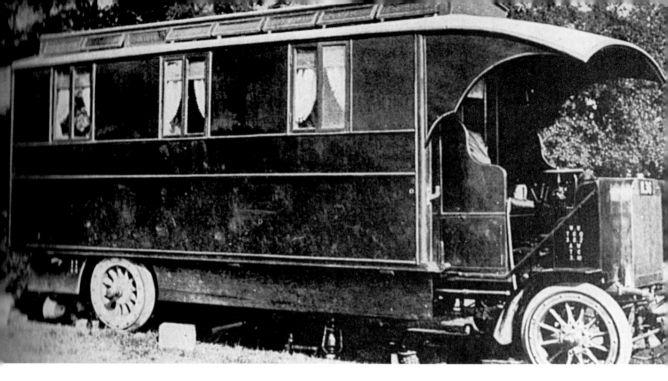

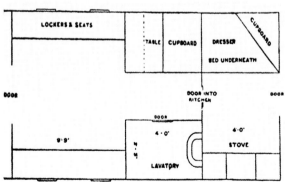

LOCKERS & SEATS

TABLE | CUPBOARD | DRESSER | CUPBOARD

BED UNDERNEATH

DOOR INTO KITCHEN

DOOR

DOOR

DOOR

9'9" | 4·0' | 4·0'

STOVE

LAVATORY

Above: *Mr Mallalieu's specially built motorhome was impressive for 1906, even J. Harris Stone was impressed – especially with the wine storage!*

Left: *Mr Mallalieu's motorhome floor plan showing the rear door; another front door took you into the cab.*

He had designed his motorhome to sleep up to six persons, so it was lavish in its design. It had a bathroom, dining room, bedroom and a kitchen – plus a loo! The motorhome also had a lantern roof design which was very popular for horse-drawn, and later car-towed, caravans. J. Harris Stone of the Caravan Club was shown round it one day, and with its staircase and impressive stock of good wines, Stone's attitude was said to soften slightly.

Mr Mallalieu's motorhome actually toured in Derbyshire. A trip to Buxton must have been an adventure with the three-speed gearbox struggling up the steep hills. A problem for early motorhome designs of this period were the roads, which were not often the best, and, of course, no official sites for stays existed. This would severely restrict the usage of motorhomes such as Mr Mallalieu's. The weight and solid rubber tyres would sink in any ground that was wet, especially with its size, although he apparently drove on to Chatsworth at a cruising speed of 9mph! Mallalieu's design didn't inspire anybody else in that period.

With all the equipment on board, which was to include oil lamps and a heavy stove and paraffin heater, the early motorhome user was in fact a camper in many ways, but with more comfort. However, they still found camping items such as tilly lamps and spades to be of great use. Large wooden blocks were also carried on a motorhome trip for parking on unlevel ground. The Camping Club published a book of hints and tips, mainly for the camping fraternity but the horse-drawn caravan user was also catered for. The motorhome user was seen as a very niche sector of the outdoor experience, but the book did have some information.

The one-off motorhome building was to carry on, with more examples being created. Some of these were crude and usually very heavy, like Mr Mallalieu's. The development of the motorhome was slow, and it is possible that any articles published on this leisure vehicle may have inspired others to improve their own design.

Earlier, in France, Monsieur Collin Dufresne of Grenoble owned a very high-quality motorhome for its time. It was double skinned using aluminium panels, and its weight was 2 tons. The 40hp Lorraine–Dietrich motor was capable of a top speed of 25mph. It was lighter and faster than Mr Mallalieu's design and yet it lacked for nothing for a touring holiday. Four rooms allowed a kitchen area, plus a room that could sleep up to five – and this included the chauffeur. The kitchen had a paraffin, removable camping stove. The motorhome also had a washroom, so it was self-contained. To add more living space, the Frenchman also had an add-on side tent (i.e. an awning), which added a massive amount of floor area and costing a whopping £1,000 – it gave him an ideal home on wheels for touring.

In the meantime, the horse-drawn caravan was becoming more popular but still only among the rich. It was able to travel over rougher tracks and could pitch up in more remote areas. The motorised caravan was still very restricted due to its weight and also its reliability. Those such as Mr Mallalieu's large motorhome were often seen using paved areas to park up. Sometimes an owner would even use a hotel parking area which was often hard standing.

The motorhome was still in its embryonic stage and those few that existed were mainly heavily underpowered, with poor handling and brakes that were often not up to stopping the weight. These crude versions were not selling 'the dream', as it were. And even if you arrived safely at your camping destination, once they were set up – which back in the early 1900s could take over an hour – if you had forgotten something, you had to walk or cycle to the nearest village shop. One early motorhome owner was reported to have fitted a towing attachment to his motorhome which enabled him to tow a small car behind for just this purpose. This idea had all the hallmarks of a disaster waiting to happen …

Fun fact: Motorhome owners were seen as eccentric in the early 1920s, with some trailer caravanners snubbing them!

One UK-built motorhome was said to be a design that could possibly turn the tide for the popularity of the vehicle. This was a special build for a director of Dunlop Tyres – Mr Arthur Du Cros – using a new Austin chassis. Although it was a large vehicle, it didn't weigh as much as Mr Mallalieu's, nor cost as much, for that matter. The Austin-based motorhome weighed in at less than 2 tons, a feat worthy of mention, and also cost just short of £2,000 in 1909. In fact, it was shown at the 1909 Motor Show and was certainly the first recorded motorhome to be shown at this venue.

The Austin-based motorhome didn't really have folk scrambling to look at it, however. Considering its build and design, this was a surprise when you viewed its specification. The body frame was ash, covered on the outside with aluminium, while the interior panelling was proper English oak. It came with a separate lounge area that could seat up to six and also act as a sleeping quarters. It had a kitchen, complete with paraffin stove, and lighting, which was provided by a 12-volt supply consisting of two on-board batteries.

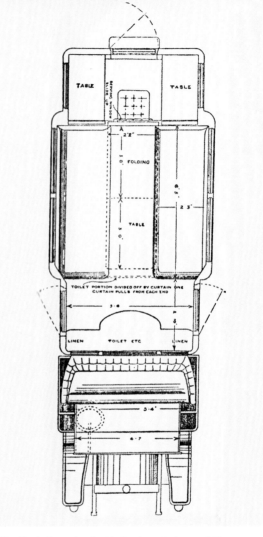

Mr Du Cros's floor plan for his Austin motorhome. A few were built at £2,000, but in 1909 it wasn't cheap!

The chauffeur had an intercom in the driving cab, which was connected through to the rear so that instructions could be given. The chauffeur and servant had a tent on the roof with steps on the side. The lantern roof design also housed two water tanks to feed the pumped water to the kitchen.

Strangely, the Austin wasn't a hit with visitors. Many seemed to think that the motorhome was a novelty – and an expensive one at that. The poor handling and limited range of these clumsy vehicles did the idea no good at all. Although the fledgling Caravan Club, with its horse-drawn caravan members, did have a motorhome or two turn up to several meets, they were seen as folk with more money than sense and perhaps a little eccentric.

In 1912, a lady named Mrs Paton had commissioned a more compact design of coach-built motorhome. This was built on a Halley chassis, with the bodywork manufactured by the Midland Counties Motor Garage in Leicester. It was powered by a 16–20hp engine. The very square design meant it gave every inch of usable space within its compact dimensions.

The roof had a contraption that was basically a roof rack. However, this made it top heavy and, unfortunately, it acquired the nickname of 'Tortoise'. It had three sections, with a room at the front that was used for sleeping, a middle room was classed as a dining area, and the next room was the kitchen. Access was via a ladder on the side or through from the cab. Storage had been important to Mrs Paton and the 'Tortoise' apparently had plenty – perhaps it was to supply long trips or provide plenty of clothing.

With no companies actively producing motorhomes, the few existing ones – in the UK especially – were built as one-offs. Without a firm to look at taking the plunge to design and then market a new leisure vehicle, the motorhome at this time wasn't going very far.

As mentioned previously, the Caravan Club meets would see the odd motorhome come along. It was reported that one became stuck at the entrance of the meet field, blocking the way for other members. The club members would not have been too bothered about this disaster for the poor motorhome owner. Many members raised the fact that these noisy contraptions worried wildlife and scared their horses too! These elite members were quite traditional in their outlook and didn't want to see the horse-drawn caravan made obsolete. However, they did not seem to realise that this was going to happen anyway with the advent of the early car-pulled caravan trailers.

The idea was also scorned by the club's founder, J. Harris Stone, who thought that the motorised caravan was detrimental to the club's ideals. 'Why,' he exclaimed, 'these motorised caravans flouted the idea of the open road. The motorhome user stopped at the best hotels with solid ground and also ate at the hotel! The motorhome owner used his leisure vehicle just to sleep in!' Stone was also keen to emphasise the slow pace of the caravanner, who often observed his surroundings as part of the holiday, while the motorhome owner sped past places of interest.

However, Stone may have been a little jealous of the distances of around 90 miles that could be covered in a full day in a motorhome, compared to 20 with a caravan …

In the UK, it was estimated that twelve to fifteen motorhomes were in private use. The French seemed to be pulling ahead, and it wouldn't be until just before 1920 that the USA also began using a chassis cab for what they called a 'house car'.

Back in the UK, in 1911 one Caravan Club meet witnessed the arrival of the Gaekwad of Baroda along with the Maharajah of Gwalior. They were considering buying horse-drawn caravans and wanted to know more. Instead, they spotted a motorhome, and soon after being shown around by the owner, they left realising that a motorhome was more in their line.

The Maharajah designed his motorhome for hunting trips on which he would invite up to sixteen guests. With his ideas, he knocked on the door of Melvin Hart, a one-time naval architect, who was building specials with his small company, Flat Van. As these were just one-off specials, this was ideal for the Maharajah who needed all the space he could have. With his luxury motorhome, it was decided that extra accommodation was needed, and this led to a four-wheel caravan being built and then pulled behind the motorhome.

The few owners of motorhomes in the UK were daring in that they also took long summer trips abroad, travelling to countries such as Belgium, Holland, France and Germany. It wasn't common, but these early users proved that it was possible to travel afar with a motorhome. One of the problems with motorhomes was that they were heavy and, as mentioned earlier, this restricted their ability to get deep into the countryside. The motorhome user had to take a large jack and usually several sturdy wooden planks. Even if the ground was solid enough at the start of the stay, the motorhome might sink in, so this selection of kit had to be carried.

There were thought to be other motorhomes built before the First World War, but more on those shortly. With the growing ownership of cars and the combustion engine being improved on all the time, there was a hint of what the next coming decades would see in leisure vehicles. The motorhome at this time was niche in every way, but the growing availability of different types and shapes of cars meant that some owners were able to convert their cars into motorhomes using a coachbuilder to add another body. However, with still no dedicated manufacturer, development was left to those early motorhome pioneers.

The Caravan Club's J. Harris Stone remarked that he would take motorhomes into the club. He explained to a member of the club that there was room enough in England for both the caravan and the motorhome.

However, the motorhome owner wanted all the trappings of home luxuries and wanted a body built in the same way as a first-class railway carriage. Mr Mallalieu's large unit had eventually taken him all around the UK, but lighter designs would need to be built.

Melvin Hart's Flat Van being inspected by a new rich American customer. Hart also built houseboats.

Stone had predicted that the motorhome would be better if it were lighter and less extravagant, which would allow better access to small roads and pitches. The club published a list of certain places where you could spend a few nights, with most of these being off the beaten track.

Around this time there was a report of a car-pulled caravan being developed – although it was perhaps more of a personal project. In early 1914, a chap named Fredrick Alcock looked at a car-pulled trailer caravan. His towing vehicle was a 1912 Lanchester. The caravan was quite ahead of its time in its profile, with a curved flat roof and square ends. It could easily have been a design from the early 1950s.

Sadly, the trailer caravan was believed to have hardly been used, and in 1969 its axle and wheels were found in a garden, so the Alcock caravan had long gone. The trailer caravan would eventually become the new must-have – but anyway, back to the motorhome story.

In 1912, a motorhome built on a Gregoire chassis was entered into the San Sebastian Rally. It had a boxy body style and was named the 'Menagerie Gregoire'. Able to do 25mph and transport up to eleven persons, it was well equipped, and the French design looked good too. It was large, but it finished the rally and beat over 100 or so other vehicles.

Also in 1912, a Mr Lomax heard of the motorised caravan and – getting what information he could – he set about designing and building one of his own using an old Panhard chassis. He had a family of four to cater for and he used an old coach house as his workshop.

The Lomax motorhome was pretty crude, and it was said that the tyres were quite 'worn' – there was no MOT back then! Within its big square body, which towered at an amazing 4m, it had a plain interior, with settees that were made into beds at night for the children, plus a fifth berth in the driver's cab. There was a kitchen area with a paraffin stove, which also gave out some heat. The family affectionately named it the 'Chalet Roulant'.

They planned a three-week tour, leaving London and reaching Maidenhead, with several onlookers mocking the 'Chalet' as it trundled out of London. The Lomax family kept a log of their days and when out in the countryside, the sight of the 'Chalet' trundling down a small lane sent a farmer's wife into hysterics, thinking she was about to be abducted. However, with the Lomax family on board she realised they were not hostile!

Mrs Lomax would usually begin preparing a meal for the next stopover, which must have been very difficult as it rolled and pitched on the move. They travelled to Devon – not an easy journey back then with a contraption like this – and they ended pitching up for a week near Babbacombe Bay in South Devon. Just imagine the memories that were made for the Lomax children on their tours, having great adventures on the way!

A year after the Lomaxes, in 1913, Bill Riley had retired from his merchant business. He was bestowed with time on his hands and looked at the great outdoors as a means of enjoying his leisure time. He looked at camping, but then didn't like the idea in poor weather. So, along with his son, Bill Riley Jnr, and his gardener, in late 1912 he

In 1913–14, Bill Riley Snr and Jnr built a coach-built on a 1909 Talbot car with the help of the gardener.

decided to convert his Talbot 1909 car to sleep in and have some living quarters. Working in an old outbuilding, the project was soon completed.

Mr Riley Snr contacted *Autocar*, the car journal, and they ran an article on this motorhome which slightly resembled a delivery van. Testing its performance, father and son were impressed and the magazine readers also took an interest, with some even wanting to buy it.

A Home-made Caravan Body.

Designed and Built by a Private Motorist for Use on a Touring Car Chassis.
Interchangeable with a Four-seater Body in Fifteen Minutes.

Above: *Old images of the Rileys' Talbot 1909 motorhome caused much interest in* Autocar Magazine.

Below: *A one-off 'special' motorhome was built for famous modern artist C.R.W. Nevinson to use as a studio in New York in the early 1920s.*

The Rileys decided to try to promote and develop their motorhome. They were approached by a Birmingham coachbuilder, who wanted to make it, and the Rileys came to an agreement.

This is where the first chapter comes to a close, with the motorhome about to be produced on a commercial scale. The Rileys would be proactive in design, manufacture and marketing, and would shape the market for the motorhome as well as the trailer caravan. Here would be the seeds for the start of an industry.

Unfortunately, the Great War would put the brakes on everything, including the Rileys, who were keen to get up and running in business. It would also be the death knell of the horse-drawn caravan as the car and trailer caravan took hold. The early 1920s would see more one-off special-build motorhomes – one such example was built for C.R.W. Nevinson, the artist, who had a motorhome constructed on a Model T Ford, to sleep two. He was to ship it to New York, where he completed some famous paintings.

2.

The Motorhome Comes of Age

The Great War came to an end in 1918, and with it a surplus of ex-army vehicles, which would be sold off to the public. In some cases, these would end up as motorhomes, but a commercial producer was needed who would also promote the virtues of the motorhome as a leisure vehicle idea.

Stepping back to 1914, the Riley father and son team had set up the manufacture of motorhomes with a coachbuilder in Birmingham. The war, however, had seen this idea flounder. Riley Snr was convinced that his idea was possibly a new venture for him and his son. With Riley Jnr now back from the services, both were looking to invest in a business of sorts.

It was in the local paper that the Rileys spotted an advert from a motor transport company looking for investors. Mr Eccles, the company owner, had let it get run down, along with its premises at Gosta Green near Birmingham. The Rileys put forward a proposal with an investment of £6,000. The company was renamed the Eccles Motor Transport Company in 1919.

Unfortunately, the lorries owned by the company had proved, on closer inspection, to be in very bad shape. The pair set to, and began

The rundown Gosta Green buildings that the Rileys purchased in 1918 where they would begin the world's first commercial caravan and motorhome production.

improving the premises, adding a new roof and repairing the lorries. With just a £3,500 turnover, the pair had to act quickly.

The motorhome idea as a commercial business was seen as a way to generate more cashflow. Riley Jnr had experienced towing trailer

ambulances in the war and also wanted to make a car-pulled caravan. This idea was to come at a time when the Caravan Club was finding it hard to survive with horse-drawn caravans – with horses taken for war work, and in some cases the caravans too, for officer accommodation. Membership had dwindled.

The motorhome and the trailer caravan was almost certainly the answer. Quickly developing a new concept and using a disused part of their premises, a much improved motorhome was built, along with a trailer caravan.

The results looked good for the time, but they needed to be sold – and quickly. The idea was to book a stand at the Olympia Motor Show in October 1919. However, with limited space, they had to hire a garage next door. As folk passed by, they definitely got some attention.

The Rileys had to sell the idea of car-pulled caravans along with the new motorhome, which looked quite modern. They also needed a brand name and Eccles was the obvious one. The pair

1920 Olympia Show: the 'Eccles Motorised Caravan', as it was described on the day, sold to Lady Dowager Viscountess Rhondda.

It was official, with this advert telling folk about their smart and up-to-date caravans and motorhomes – it says, 'The Motor Caravan People'!

CARAVANS

SMART AND UP-TO-DATE

.... BY ....

ECCLES MOTOR TRANSPORT

LIMITED

7, 8 and 9, Gosta Green
and 1 to 6, Lister Street

BIRMINGHAM

Telephone CENTRAL 472

"THE MOTOR CARAVAN PEOPLE"

.... and ....

GENERAL BODY BUILDERS

 Caravan on Ford - - - Chassis - - -

As Supplied to CHURCH ARMY & MINISTRY OF HEALTH

11 feet long, 7 feet wide, and 6 feet 6 inches high.

FOR PLEASURE OR FOR PROPAGANDA WORK

CONTAINS Stove, Wardrobe, Dresser, Washstand, 3 Tables, Lockers. Sleeping accommodation for 4 persons.

BUILT in our usual high-class manner, with nothing but best material and finish.

CONSTRUCTED of rolled sheet-metal covering, with interior of specially selected french polished figured wood.

Mollycroft in Roof and large extending Platform at back.

PRICES ON APPLICATION.

Eccles built on most chassis, but they were keen on using the 1-ton Ford.

sold their products at the motor show and it was then they decided that they could move into full production, so a factory area was set up. The Eccles motorhome and trailer caravan was now in production. Enquiries would come in for motorhomes to be designed and adapted for use by travelling clergy and other organisations on a 1-ton Ford chassis.

Eccles would build many 'specials', learning more about design and construction as they went on.

This Eccles was built for a business that made health pills. It
accommodated three adults.

The Rileys could build on virtually any chassis cab, new or used. With further advertising and their hire fleets expanding, by the early 1920s production was increasing. Building 'specials' also proved to be excellent at spreading the Eccles name in motorhomes, but also motorhome usage in general.

A travelling family of chemists, who wanted an office, home and workshop, ordered a 'special' that was built on an AEC 4-ton lorry chassis. The motorhome was built using ash-frame bodywork and oak panelling inside, with beaten steel for the exterior panelling. It was well designed, and furniture was built using oak veneer. It was a truly lavish motorhome for 1928. The owners could also make up their pills in another section of the Eccles, then drive around selling them (how times have changed!).

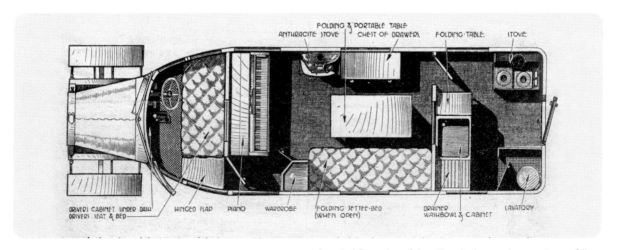

Detailed floor plan of the pill-maker's motorhome – it was fully equipped for the time (around 1928).

Eccles customers were wealthy and would travel to places far and wide on adventures and then write and praise Eccles' design and workmanship. (Photo courtesy of John Lowe)

Extending platform on rear of a 1920s motorhome with sun lounge, which was then taken down in sections when it was time to move on!

1920 motorhome which, amusingly, dismantled and stored away so that the lorry could be given back to its owner!

Various owners wrote to Eccles, telling them how their motorhomes had proved very comfortable. Many travelled great distances abroad, spreading the Eccles word, with sales being made in India and around the world.

However, with one commercial make now available, it was inevitable that a few small manufacturing concerns would pop up by the early 1920s, mainly making trailer caravans but also a few motorhomes, including Winchester, Car Cruiser, Raven, Summerfield (later Cheltenham Caravans) – and, of course, there were plenty of home-builds also surfacing.

Some owners would make alterations to a production motorhome by adding a sun lounge extension when pitched! In 1921, one chap bought a 3.9m x 1.95m caravan then borrowed a lorry and transferred the caravan to the back of it. He, his wife and three children claimed it was a fine motorhome. He gave the lorry back after the summer break and took the caravan off in sections and stored them in his shed!

The motorhome market that had begun to exist in the early 1920s was basically dominated by Eccles as the Rileys improved their designs and used various chassis. The trailer caravan had become the most popular of the two formats, with increased car ownership as well as more powerful and reliable engines and better roads.

J. Harris Stone of the Caravan Club was most impressed by a lightweight motorhome that was designed and owned by Mr Appleton from Weston-super-Mare, in the West Country, in the early 1920s. It caused great interest on Caravan Club meets because of its design with

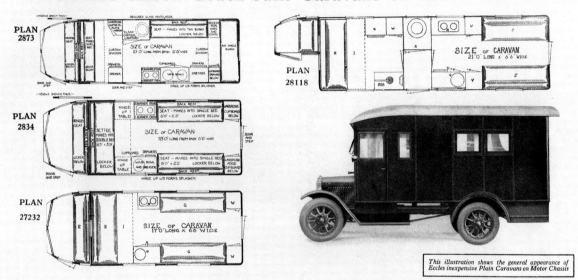

ECCLES Saloon Coach-built Caravans on Motor Chassis

This illustration shows the general appearance of Eccles inexpensive Plain Caravans on Motor Chassis

PRICES. COMPLETELY FURNISHED AND FITTED.

Prices subject to Chassis being complete	Plan 2834 For 5 people	Plan 27232 For 5 people	Plan 2873 For 5 people in two compartments	Plan 28118 For 6 people in two compartments
	£	£	£	£
De Luxe Saloon Coach-built Caravans (see illustration on page 24)				
Panelled in Steel Armoured Plywood, Light Polish	410	370	550	560
Ditto, in Jacobean coloured Oak Polish, with leaded windows ..	440	400	580	590
Double Walls extra in each case	30	30	40	40
Aluminium Armoured Plywood extra in each case	20	20	30	30

All suitable for Large Bus or Commercial Chassis

INEXPENSIVE PLAIN BUILT CARAVANS

for mounting on chassis similar in plan to our plain model Trailer Caravans with enclosed saloon drive.

Panelled in Steel Armoured Plywood, Light Polish, to sleep three £175

Panelled in Steel Armoured Plywood, Light Polish, to sleep four £207

Mudguards, pan boxes and mounting charges extra, according to chassis.

(See illustration of general appearance above)

By the mid-1920s, Eccles were cleverly designing motorhome ranges with new layouts. The cost for the top model was over £600.

its full, all-round blind canopies – it was named the 'Aeroplane'.

Appleton had been a camper but had begun looking at motorhomes. He drew sketches of his design with its 3m body length, and then had it built. It was designed for two, but with more folk on a tour, a tent was needed as well. This lightweight motorhome was to impress Harris Stone, who saw potential in this type of design. Hiring a motorhome could cost around £9 a week, but private individuals were hesitant because of the cost, access difficulties and having no experience of driving anything bigger than a car. Being able to pitch up in more remote areas, and more easily driven, this type of smaller motorhome could become popular.

Eccles built mainly on Morris chassis, but the Model T Ford was also used, making more compact motorhomes that were affordable. The Rileys were ahead of the game, and success saw the transport side sold off while they invested their time and money in new premises, with demand for their caravans and motorhomes now high.

A typical motorhome interior from Eccles showing good storage and seating.

A full awning around Appleton's motorhome earned it the name 'Aeroplane'! It was a sight to behold in the early 1920s.

Mr Appleton's motorhome – he attended several Caravan Club meets where its lighter weight compared to normal examples impressed members.

ECCLES Saloon Coach-built Caravans on Motor Chassis

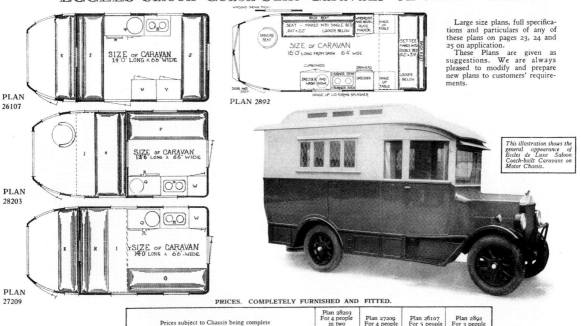

PLAN 26107

SIZE OF CARAVAN
14'0" LONG x 66" WIDE

PLAN 2892

WINDOWS SHOWN THUS:—

BACK REST
SEAT — MAKES INTO SINGLE BED
60" x 22"   LOCKER BELOW

WARDROBE AND BEVEL PLATE MIRROR

HINGE UP TABLE

DRIVERS SEAT

SIZE OF CARAVAN
15'0" LONG FROM DASH   64" WIDE

SETTEE MAKES INTO DOUBLE BED 62" x 59"

CUPBOARDS   DRAWERS

DRESSER AND WASH BOWL

2 BURNER STOVE

DRESSER   HINGE UP TABLE

LOCKER BELOW

1 BURNER OVEN

DOOR AND STEP   HINGE UP LID FORMS SPLASHER

Large size plans, full specifications and particulars of any of these plans on pages 23, 24 and 25 on application.

These Plans are given as suggestions. We are always pleased to modify and prepare new plans to customers' requirements.

PLAN 28203

SIZE OF CARAVAN
14'6" LONG x 66" WIDE

This illustration shows the general appearance of Eccles de Luxe Saloon Coach-built Caravans on Motor Chassis.

PLAN 27209

SIZE OF CARAVAN
14'0" LONG x 66" WIDE

PRICES. COMPLETELY FURNISHED AND FITTED.

Prices subject to Chassis being complete	Plan 28203 For 4 people in two compartments*	Plan 27209 For 4 people *	Plan 26107 For 5 people *	Plan 2892 For 3 people †
	£	£	£	£
De Luxe Saloon Coach-built Caravans (see illustration on page 24)				
Panelled in Steel Armoured Plywood, Light Polish	280	290	295	340
Ditto, in Jacobean coloured Oak Polish, with leaded windows..	295	305	310	360
Double Walls extra in each case	20	20	20	25

Eccles had, by the late 1920s, increased the layouts and variations of its motorhome ranges. They stated that they would make alterations to any if requested.

UPLANDS CARAVANS

HIRE SERVICE

" Uplands Service " aims at nothing short of perfection.

The equipment provided (see list herewith) is unusually complete, both as to bedding, cooking and washing facilities, cutlery, table-ware and linen, storage accommodation, and sanitary provisions.

The knowledge and experience of the Directors will be enthusiastically put at the disposal of every party. Routes will be planned free of charge, camping-places indicated, and no pains spared to make the tour a memorable one for all concerned. Capable driver-attendants can be supplied, if desired.

TERMS

(Minimum Hire Period, two Weeks)

July, August and September	... per week	£11 11	0
June	... ,,	10 10	0
April and May ...	... ,,	9 9	0
October to March ...	... Terms on application.		

Special quotations for long periods.

INSURANCE.—The Hirer must insure through the Owners under a Comprehensive Policy, at the rates given under " Hiring Conditions".

For Hiring Conditions see back page.

The Uplands Hire information sheet. They would supply a driver if required, plan routes and stopovers. Two weeks' hire cost £11.

Notable journeys with Eccles motorhomes included a 10,000-mile trip with the owners taking their servants and travelling through various continents, with a 1932 Eccles De-Luxe motorhome on a Chevrolet chassis. This was a tough journey back then and made these folk truly motorhome pioneers.

The motorhome users would tell of their travels and the sights they had encountered. Don't forget that, at this time, the UK had many villages and hamlets that were unspoilt and still as they had been for many years. Doctors reported that out-of-doors camping was ideal for one's health and well-being, and this further enhanced the potential of motorhome ownership.

The motorhome and trailer caravan was still a rich person's hobby, but now instead of having to search around for a coachbuilder to help you put together a motorhome – usually at great expense – the selection of small manufacturers springing up would help to bring the cost down. Another important factor was the speeding up of development.

These pioneer motorhome users did a 10,000-mile round trip – leopard skins and monkeys were some of the souvenirs they came back with! (Photo courtesy of John Lowe)

By the late 1920s Eccles had a purpose-built factory for motorhome and caravan production – the first in the world.

However, the self-build DIY motorhome was still very much in evidence, with most people using old car chassis. One notable one was a Mr Nathan, who, in several months, used a car chassis to build a hefty body which could sleep his family of four. A primus camping stove and electric lighting with sprung seats and a decent finish meant this 1924 self-build was a good one. It featured in a local newspaper, and by 1925 he was off touring with his family to prove what a decent job had been done. Mr and Mrs Nathan visited many areas of the UK, including Worcestershire and the far north.

Eccles were leading in design and influencing others on the way. Wilkinson Cox was a motor trader and built a motorhome in the 1920s. He sold it and decided to build another, again using a Model T Ford as a base. He also sold this one. He started his company, Raven Caravans, and the motorhomes were replaced with the manufacture of trailer caravans. The Caravan Club was now seeing more trailer caravans, with the horse-drawn ones phasing out. The motorhome was making more of an appearance on club meets but the trailer was more popular.

Bertram Hutchings, the founder of Winchester Caravans, moved into building motorhomes. They resembled their trailer caravans but were on four wheels instead of two. The Hutchings motorhomes varied in size and chassis used, and no set pattern would emerge from this quality builder, who would build exactly to customers' requirements, so the price was high. But Hutchings would lean to his trailer caravans which resembled the old horse-drawn design.

In 1927, a company called Upland Caravans, based in London, began building on Ford 1-ton chassis. This square, box-like motorhome could be built to various specifications: it could be a basic shell, or fully equipped. Named the 'Eagle', the four-berth version was £320, while the basic was £298 – the price also depended on chassis and age. The driver was self-contained in his cab, away from the living area, which was

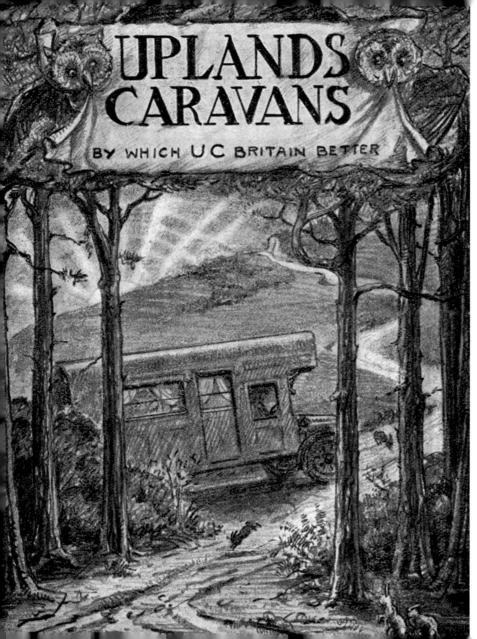

UPLANDS
CARAVANS

BY WHICH UC BRITAIN BETTER

Upland Caravans claimed that their motorhomes enabled you to see Britain better — they sold and hired the Upland motorhome.

double panelled, using mahogany for the interior walls. The Eagle had two halves – one included the bunks at the rear, while the other had a free-standing table and four chairs to it. Upland hired out the Eagle for £22 a week, but also sold direct to the public.

Another milestone in design came from designer and manufacturer, Road Yacht. The Light Cruiser was a modern, streamlined design that looked unusual with its curved roofline and profile. It could be built on any chassis but needed an engine of over 20hp. The claim that it was car-like to drive may not have been entirely true! Even in standard trim it was very luxurious, costing just over £500 in the 1920s. It was lavish, with an electric cooker and heater, hot water and two 20-gallon water tanks. It had a gramophone, radio, loo/shower, plug sockets and even an ice-making machine. Powered windscreen wipers and traffic indicators were other features that made it far ahead of its time, with a slogan 'The future today'. Sadly, it didn't take off and the firm stopped building them.

The Upland Eagle motorhome. Looking through the front cab, the rear bunkbeds and free-standing table can be just seen.

Another maker who would also begin with motorhomes was Car Cruiser. Its founder and owner, Major Fleming Williams, began building his first motorhome in the 1920s, but with little success, so trailer caravans were to be Car Cruiser's main business. They were noted for their extreme streamlined profiles, earning Williams the nickname of 'Streamlined Bill'.

VIEW OF GALLEY
SHOWING SINK
SECURED OVER STOVE.

VIEW OF GALLEY
SHOWING STOVE
CLEAR OF SINK.

VIEW ON BOWS.

VIEW OF WASH BASIN
AND LAVATORY.

VIEW OF WASH
BASIN.

The mid-1920s Road Yacht was the super-streamlined luxury motorhome of its day. Its cab was part of the body, a sort of A-class of the 1920s.

* * *

Memories: John Lowe – This journal of an affluent couple's 10,000-mile trip in an Eccles De-Luxe motorhome, with images, turned up at a Derbyshire auction! I managed to purchase the incredible journal of the trip from 1934. The Fullers took their maid, Mary, on the trip, which included a journey through the Sahara and getting stuck in a sand dune. They returned safely. What a great trip that must have been!

However, back to Eccles, because they really did, by the mid-1920s, become masters of motorhome design and manufacture. The Rileys had also been building special trucks – i.e. new bodies on old and new chassis. From horse boxes and small cattle trailers, the company also built special motorhomes for various organisations. They also built motorhome mobile display units for brands such as Philips, Persil and many others. Eccles Motor Caravans, as they were now branded, had moved into larger premises by the end of the 1920s, expanding their buildings as sales increased in trailer caravans and motorhomes.

They were way ahead of the game with their forward-thinking designs, but marketing was another strong area as Eccles were seen more and more in both the local and national press promoting caravanning and motorhomes. The trailer was becoming more popular, but what market existed in motorhomes was taken by Eccles. Using Ford and Morris chassis, Eccles were flexible enough to come up with different layouts for their models and they also offered both a standard and deluxe range, offering more luxury for those who could afford it, with a higher grade finish and more expensive styling.

Fun fact: One motorhome owner was mistaken for a delivery van!

47

Eccles used their motorhome experience to build 'specials' such as this Philips Radio Promotions lorry in the late 1920s.

The Eccles factory at Stirchley was the first purpose-built caravan and motorhome production plant in the world. The Rileys were very organised, with different production areas with several models being worked on at once, fed by various stores within the factory. Nobody could touch them in many respects.

* * *

Some trailer caravan users were not happy towing, especially on bad roads. Lady Lamington from South Lanarkshire had bought a trailer caravan from London – make not known – and she had her chauffeur to tow it. She wrote in a journal that she had become fed up with the trailer caravan rattling on the roads, so she took it to a local garage. She then instructed the garage owner to put the caravan body on a Ford 1-ton chassis. Lady Lamington noted how much better the now-motorised caravan behaved and in April 1924, with maid and chauffeur, she set off to go south.

She instructed her chauffeur to look out for inns or hotels to park up for the night or stop over for lunch. She noted how easy the travel was and wherever she stopped, folk asked questions about its price and comfort and where could they buy one. What a sight it must have been to see this coming down through a village.

The lighting was by electricity and the stove was paraffin, but she carefully noted the fuel she purchased as some types would smell too strong. One morning, she woke up to several inches of snow but maintained that her motorhome was still snug.

She travelled through Yorkshire, stopping at hotels and sleeping in the van on the car park. She also noted that a price of 2 shillings a night was charged at one site and remarked it wasn't an official price! Lady Lamington travelled through the Yorkshire Dales and noted the lovely inns on the way. It sounds as though she never cooked a meal in the converted motorhome and basically had meals in these establishments instead.

Opposite: *Motorhome production at the Stirchley factory was very advanced for 1929.*

Above: *Several internal departments at the factory meant production was kept flowing. This is the upholstery department.*

The Lamingtons, with their chauffeur and maid, ready for a tour in 1924 to the south of England.

Lady Lamington kept a diary of their trip and the folk they met. This is at the White Lion Inn at Kildwick –they stopped off for a meal.

The best meal of the trip was at the White Lion at the village of Kildwick, near Skipton. No hotel or inn had suitable places to park the motorhome in Skipton itself, but the White Lion had a firm spot and made her most welcome.

She noted how the engine had cut out and the chauffeur was given the job to repair it. Then, how an AA scout had turned up and wouldn't fix it until Lady Lamington promised to join! The journey took four days to arrive at London, seeing her relations on the way at various country houses – what a way to spend leisure time in a period of the mid-1920s when most of the UK was still untouched in rural and small seaside areas.

Fun fact: Most motorhome owners had a chauffeur, who was expected to repair the vehicle too!

* * *

This motorhome owner has an off-the-beaten-track pitch; note the blocks under the rear to level it.

These two motorhomes from the 1920s have been pitched and not moved in years. They are being used as 'static' caravans.

As the 1920s turned into the 1930s, the motorhome began to lose its pace against trailer caravans, with mostly 'specials' being built. Levelling a motorhome was still a problem, even with the lighter designs of the late 1920s; this still required wooden chocks, especially on wild, uneven ground. Motorhome hire was being overtaken by trailer caravans and some of the motorhomes built in the very early 1920s would end up staying on a pitch and never moving again.

Above: *A 1933 'special' motorhome with upstairs bedroom. The owner was Captain J.F. McMullen, who used it until 1940.*

Right: *Interior shots of the McMullens' motorhome – bedroom and a lounge area offered luxury living.*

Some orders were for customers who wanted a mobile hunting lodge. In 1933, one was designed for Captain J.F. McMullen. It was basically like a double-decker bus! (In fact, by the late 1930s motorhome design would take on the profile of a single-decker bus!) Apparently, the captain's motorhome was used for Second World War work and was stripped of its fittings, which were replaced with seats. It wasn't heard of after the war, so it's possible it could have been scrapped.

There were those who travelled abroad with their motorhomes and had tales of getting stuck or having to build a raft to cross rivers! Some motorhome adventurers who went to wilder countries would come back with souvenirs. Not the sort of thing we would buy, however – no, they came back with live monkeys and animal skins! All scary stuff, but the motorhome was catching on in the USA, over trailers, while, in Europe, trailer caravans were still selling well.

Talking of adventures, in the early 1920s an English lady, Eva Hasell, had set up home in the Canadian outback with a fleet of Ford motorhomes. These were used by ministers to spread the gospel, while still having the comforts of home. Her success saw her still there in the mid-1940s, having ordered more US Ford V8-based motorhomes.

The 1930s would see more 'special' motorhome builds and as mentioned, they ran along the lines of coaches or double-decker buses. One luxury model in 1933 was basically a double-decker bus design but with complete living accommodation. Built by the firm Crerar's, of Crieff in Scotland, this was a luxury motorhome.

Eccles was still building luxury models and motorhome 'specials' for firms around this time. The 1932 Caravan Rally at Minehead saw several outfits, but only around nine motorhomes attended. A motorhome club had been formed but the trailer caravan membership still superseded motorhome owners.

In Sandbach, Cheshire, Jennings had begun making caravans, but the coachbuilders moved on to motorhomes and by the 1960s would become a well-respected luxury motorhome manufacturer.

Making 'specials' for motorhome owners carried on until the late 1930s. One was for a Mr Shurey, who in 1938 designed a motorhome that looked quite modern for its time and was built using a 1-ton Commer delivery vehicle. Mr and Mrs Shurey were often stopped so that folk could have a look at this modern-looking motorhome. After the Second World War it travelled around the UK, and when the Shureys died, their grandson took it on, last using it in the early 1970s.

> **Fun fact:** Servants were often taken on trips, and they had only a tent to stay in, no matter what the weather!

By 1939, with war looming, the small caravan industry would come to a stop. This basically saw the end of the motorhome, although some did make it into war work. Carlight, who had made luxury caravans, also built motorhome 'specials' even up to 1940. One was built for Mr Claude Dampier and his wife and daughter, who toured the UK with their motorhome, which they named 'Mrs Gibson'!

Field Marshall Montgomery apparently had a mobile office which also allowed some sleeping accommodation, and so some motorhomes would get laid up for such use during the war, or even lived in as trailer caravans. Manufacturers mainly turned to war work – Eccles had great success in manufacturing various trailers and ambulances.

* * *

A Scottish-built 'special', made around 1933 and based on a double-decker bus.

Opposite: *Mr and Mrs Shureys' late 1930s self-build motorhome, which was being used till the early 1970s.*

Below: *Mr Dampier with a Carlight-built motorhome from 1940, in which he, his wife and daughter toured the UK.*

So, this chapter comes to an end. After the conflict, any remaining motorhomes were mainly home built but unfortunately, they were taxed more than a car. In the late 1940s, St Albans Drive Hire had a few coach-built motorhomes, which it hired out.

What was needed for growth in the motorhome market was a smaller chassis to build on, but none were really available. However, the mid-1950s saw larger van designs, using car engines and gearboxes, which made them more car-like to drive. They were now also taxed as a car. New designs would also provide new bases, which would help to bring the idea of motorhome living back to the fore.

The period was going to see a new breed of motorhome – those that were converted vans. Westfalia, the German maker, for instance, took the VW Transporter and adapted it so that it could be used as a camper (although, in fact, the term 'camper van' came into being later). The labelling of vans with living accommodation as 'commercial' was dropped so the speed limit could be raised from 20mph to 30mph! However, we'll go back to the coach-built motorhome in the next chapter.

3.

The Motorhome Makes a Comeback

Shortages in the early 1950s saw that anyone wanting a coach-built motorhome would have to look hard for one. Some would even approach boat builders to build a motorhome for them. Otherwise, it was necessary to take a different approach, as I spoke of in the previous chapter. The new commercial delivery vans such as the Morris J2 and Austin J2, followed by the Bedford CA, were available in short and long wheel bases, with sliding side doors, and could also be obtained as a chassis for special bodywork, making them ideal to be converted into campers.

However, the UK, which is where the motorhome was first commercially built and marketed, would see a motorhome boom in years to come, but in the meantime, fuel prices and shortages hampered any motorhome comeback.

Fun fact: When the Caravan Club asked its members about allowing motorhomes into the club there was uproar among members, with some writing strong letters to the club.

It's at this point that the name Dormobile would emerge. Martin Walter was a long-time coachbuilder, mainly for cars at his company based in Folkestone, Kent. It would begin by converting a Morris J van for sleeping two people after a director had watched folk sleeping in their cars while waiting for the ferry. They were basic to begin with, but within a few years the Dormobile name would take the campervan (and, to an extent, the coach-built motorhome) into the public eye. So much so that any campervan or motorhome was known as a Dormobile, even if it wasn't!

The 1950s was to see the van conversion really take off, with ingenious designs to allow extra headroom and extra berths. There was definitely now a buyer for this type of leisure vehicle. You could argue that this basically got the coach-built motorhome back on the go.

The new vans/chassis cabs of the mid-1950s would help to bring back the popularity of the motorhome, as they were modern and more car-like to drive than the old lorry chassis.

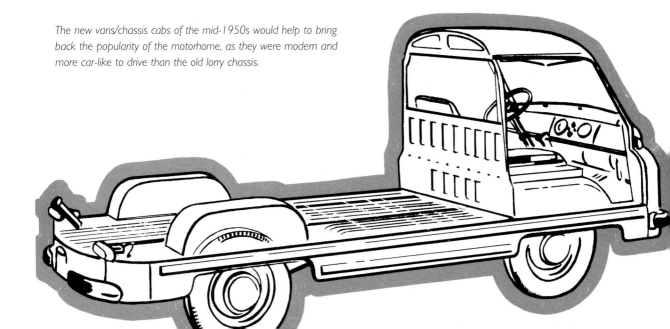

With Eccles now out of the running, making caravans only, there were new makers who started up with van conversions. In the 1950s the likes of the Ford Thames van appeared and, with Dormobile inventing a glass-fibre elevating roof, other small concerns jumped on the same ideas with various different takes on Dormobile's roof.

Car garages also began selling campervan conversions. Those who towed a caravan and fancied the idea of one vehicle to sleep and cook in would sometimes buy a van conversion and still tow a caravan behind.

The van conversions were ingenious and utilised the space very well, with specially designed kitchen and seating areas. However, for more than two they were quite cramped, to say the least. Users liked to take off just for weekends or one-night stopovers. As caravan parks began to develop after the war this meant campervans could use site facilities.

However, there were a number of people who wanted the caravan comforts but in a motorised design, the same, in fact, as Eccles had developed in the 1920s. In 1955, Central Garages based at Bradford, who also did coach building, looked at making a high-class coach-built motorhome. The problem was, this was at a time when sales generally had slumped due to the Suez Canal Crisis, out in the Middle East, putting the price of fuel up in the UK. Large-engine car sales took a dive and, therefore, making a coach-built motorhome wasn't an ideal plan. But Hobson, the owner and designer, wanted a real motorised caravan with quality furniture and space plus a loo and the new one came with two water tanks, fresh and waste.

The Hobson motorhome was named after its premises, Paralanian, and was built on an Austin 152. It became a success, in luxury terms, and opened up a new market for the coach-built motorhome. It had good lines and was also insulated in the full-spec model. A convector gas heater was fitted, as well as a battery for lighting. It cost £1,250 and was launched as a production model at the 1958 Motor Show at Earls Court (pre-Caravan & Motorhome Show days).

Eccles had, by the end of the 1930s, stopped motorhome production and just built 'specials' to order, but that also eventually dried up.

*The campervan would evolve out of the new delivery vans such
as the Ford Thames and Bedford CA and Commer.*

The 1958 Austin 152-based Paralanian had a 1.5 litre-petrol engine and cost £1,250. Its luxury trim included a heater, battery and chemical loo. It was the first commercially built motorhome on the UK market.

This opened up sales, but it was still only accessible for those who were not limited to a budget. They had originally been designed for retired couples, but some were ordered with two extra berths so that more privileged families could use them.

The increased sales proved that coach-built motorhomes were the way forward for many to enjoy more space than in a van conversion. But a really affordable motorhome was needed, and luckily one was on its way. In Poole, Dorset, Bluebird caravans had been building caravans (named the Midland) in the 1930s. Although they were cheap in build and price, by the early 1950s the owners (the Knotts) had improved their quality and now also built caravans for living in, as well as tourers, horseboxes and delivery vans.

The late 1930s saw Midland Caravans become Bluebird after the Second World War. They built living caravans, holiday caravans and tourers. By 1959 they had launched the Bluebird Highwayman at an affordable price of £875.

The 1958 Paralanian's deluxe interior was luxurious in finish and spec and boasted Axminster carpets!

Memories: Clive Brown – My parents borrowed a 1938 Austin 18 chassis with a coach-built caravan body. I was 11, and when my parents brought home the motorhome to go to North Wales on holiday, I remember travelling from Surrey to Snowdonia via Ross-on-Wye – it was a great adventure! Great days, and we could pull up where we wanted for a brew.

Clive Brown's memories.

Bill Knott heard of the Paralanian and looked at building a coach-built version too, but at a more affordable cost. In late 1958, the Bluebird motorhome, also built on an Austin 152 chassis base, came out of the factory costing £875 and sleeping more than the Paralanian. Its design was ideal for the hire market and the now-named Highwayman looked good and was well priced. It came with on-board water tank and electric lighting and was to be sold through Croft Garages, who became a main Bluebird motorhome dealership. By the early 1960s the Highwayman was selling well.

The Highwayman had a good appeal to many new motorhome folk. By 1966 it was available on the Commer chassis and by the 1970s was available on a Ford chassis, too.

Motorhome owners and campervan users had now seen their Caravan Club membership slide, with club members banning them both after a vote by its members. Luckily, private-run sites had added some more level pitches and harder standing so the motorhome was slowly seeing more acceptance.

The Bluebird Highwayman opened up the motorhome market for the coach-built motorhome, making it affordable and ideal for hire fleets.

MODELS CONVERTED	Austin 152. (coach built)
SEATING	Up to SEVEN.
BERTHS	FOUR adults.
DOORS	Rear.
FITTINGS	Wardrobe, cupboard, lockers, table, sink, cooker, water tank, electric and gas light, venetian blinds, lino.
CANOPY	Rigid 'High Top'.
FINISH	Duotone.

HIGHWAYMAN
and also COMMER 'MOTOPLUS'

Illustration shows 'Highwayman' coach-built model on Austin 152 chassis.

By the late 1960s, the Highwayman was selling well and was to become available on other chassis, and Parkstone became a major motorhome production plant.

Alternative Scheme:
Double Burner Hot Plate and
Grill with Astral Refrigerator
under.

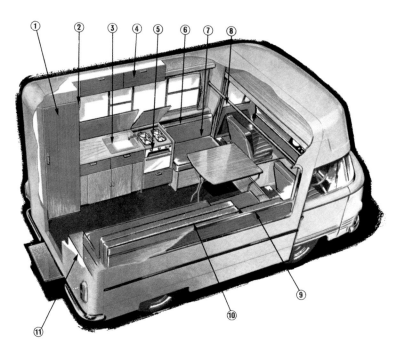

1. Wardrobe, converts to Toilet area.
2. Gas Light.
3. Sink and Drainer with Whale foot pump fed from 10 gallon under-floor tank.
4. Overhead Storage Locker.
5. Oven Cooker with storage under.
6. Table storage (behind seat back).
7. Dinette forms small double Bed. (Provided under seats are gas bottle compartment—offside, and storage compartment—nearside.)
8. Single Hammock Bunk position. Large storage compartment over cab.
9. Removable seat backs form centre panels of bed.
10. Pull-out double Bed/Settee with storage under.
11. Drawers with storage cupboard above.

B Bluebird

The DIY owner would often buy an old ambulance which was coach-built and convert it to a motorhome. This practice carried on well into the 1970s. DIY motorhomes were still mainly van conversions, but in motorhome magazines there was the odd article about those who had taken twelve months to design and build a coach-built motorhome. Some were impressive, while others were less so!

The 1960s saw another new maker join the coach-built side. This was Hadrian, in the north-east. This was another luxury coach-built, with its entrance door on the side and not at the rear, making it more caravan-like, and it attracted caravanners towards the virtues of motorhome living instead.

However, not all coach-builts were conventional. The Caraboot was made from a Mini-van and was one such design. Using glass-fibre mouldings, it all fitted together and worked on the road as an articulated vehicle. Sadly, it didn't sell. Another Mini-based coach-built was from Sussex maker, Mongoose;

costing over £1,200 in 1968, sales again proved restricted.

With consumer spending on the increase in the 1960s, touring caravans saw a sales boom. The motorhome would also witness more popularity and, with the Motor Caravanners' Club and the Camping & Caravanning Club now in support of the motorhome and campervan, this further increased interest in ownership. *Caravan Magazine* and *Modern Caravan Magazine* supported motorhome manufacturers, running tests and providing general PR, with readers sending in their stories of where to go with a motorhome.

More dedicated motorhome dealerships set up, with two being very prominent in the 1960s and '70s. First was Wilson's, a car dealer who turned to selling campervans and motorhomes in London. Its owner, Leslie Wilson, had brought all his family into the business which proved a big success. Wilson had been heavily involved in motorhomes, using them for main holidays, including continental tours (this had increased in popularity with motorhome users in the 1960s).

The market expanding with another luxury maker, Hadrian, would appeal to caravanners who wanted a motorhome with the space and fittings of a tourer.

HADRIAN

MODELS (COACH BUILT)	Austin 152. Bedford CAL. Commer 15 cwt.
SEATING	up to EIGHT.
BERTHS	FOUR adults.
DOORS	Side.
FITTINGS	Wardrobe, lockers, cupboards, drawers, table, sink, cooker, cold storage locker, Formica work-top, water storage tank, waste water tank, calor gas cylinder, two electric lights, curtains, chemical toilet compartment.
CANOPY	None (Rigid high-top).
FINISH	Single or duotone.

Illustration shows Hadrian de luxe coach-built model on Bedford long wheelbase 15 cwt. chassis

Also caravan CONVERSIONS on Austin 152, Morris J2, Bedford Long Wheelbase, Thames 15 cwt. and Standard 'Atlas Major'.

A strange idea, and expensive one to develop, was this Mini-van with coach-built glass-fibre attachment. It was named the Caraboot, but it didn't find favour.

Another micro-motorhome was the Mongoose, again using a Mini-van as its base – but its £1,200 price tag in 1968 saw low sales.

*From a small car sales dealership, Wilson's became a big
motorhome and campervan dealership – this PR image shows
the Wilson family in the late 1960s.*

The Wilsons in the Woburn Abbey grounds at a 150-motorhome vehicle rally. It was a first. They also organised a continental one in August 1965.

would continue to be the case years later, with US designs mostly being used by film companies rather than private buyers.

The US market had been very motorhome driven and by the early 1950s, several manufacturers were building models for an expanding market. New coach-built motorhomes were to evolve in the USA in the 1960s, while old UK makers such as Jennings came back with some strong designs using several different makers' bases.

Fun fact: One motorhome owner was asked if he was an ice cream van!

The Wilsons became involved with their customers, organising rallies for them and also financially supporting them on rallies. Their empire grew and by the late 1960s they had several depots. Wilson's also imported the US Winnebago motorhome for a time. It was a design that found little favour in the UK, and this

Land Rover had seen its long wheelbase being used by two makers to be converted into campervans. In 1967 Jennings went a stage further and made a coach-built motorhome using the Land Rover. Jennings would be become part of Central Garage in Bradford, which was bought out by Lookers Car Group and later ERF.

Jennings continued making motorhomes, and meanwhile Paralanian was taken over by Spen Dalesman Caravans, although by 1968 the company had gone. Then, an ex-Paralanian employee set up European Caravans (also in Bradford) and based a luxury model on the Paralanian design, naming it the Torstar. One couple who purchased one toured Europe for a month and found the Torstar practical and luxurious, but sadly the firm fell by the wayside by the early 1970s.

The new and small concerns setting up at this time are too numerous to mention in detail in this book, so I will try and keep to the main ones. One such company was Cotswold Motorhomes, owned by caravan dealer Ken Stephens, near Cheltenham. They built luxury units using the Austin J2.

Bluebird had become a giant company in 1963, as did Sprite caravans, who had taken over Eccles Caravans in 1960. Sprite/Eccles eventually took over Bluebird, renaming the concern as Caravans International. This meant that as a company they now produced motorhomes, campervans, tourers, static caravans and park homes, making them the biggest leisure vehicle manufacturer in the world. After several years, the CI Group had purchased several companies – the motorhome side even produced a Sprite coach-built using the 1965-launched Ford Transit Custom – unlike its caravan sibling, the Sprite motorhome was a luxury model but unfortunately sales were slow.

Dormobile was to move into coach-built motorhomes in a different way, using glass-fibre body moulds and introducing a very eye-catching and stylish motorhome. Introduced in 1964, it was distinctive and based on a Bedford CA. The Debonair was a hit and over the years it was tweaked and remained popular. Production was quite intense, but the sales proved it was worth it, making the Debonair a sought-after motorhome years later.

From 1967, the Caravan Club reluctantly allowed motorhome owners to become members, although the motorhome owner was still seen as an outcast by some caravanners. The motorhome market was growing (14,000 sold in 1973) and dealerships emerged and grew.

Below: *An unusual motorhome conversion by Jennings on a Land Rover in the late 1960s. It was a short-lived model.*

Opposite: *European Caravans was set up by an ex-Paralanian boss and copied the same format – luxury, well-built motorhomes. They were named Torstar.*

The Cotswold motorhome was built by Ken Stephens near Cheltenham.
This later became caravan dealers Golden Castle Leisure. They were
well built and beautifully finished yet practical motorhomes.

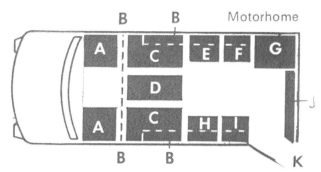

Motorhome

CIM was the name of the CI Bluebird Motorhome Division – the Sprite Ford Transit-based motorhome was launched in 1965.

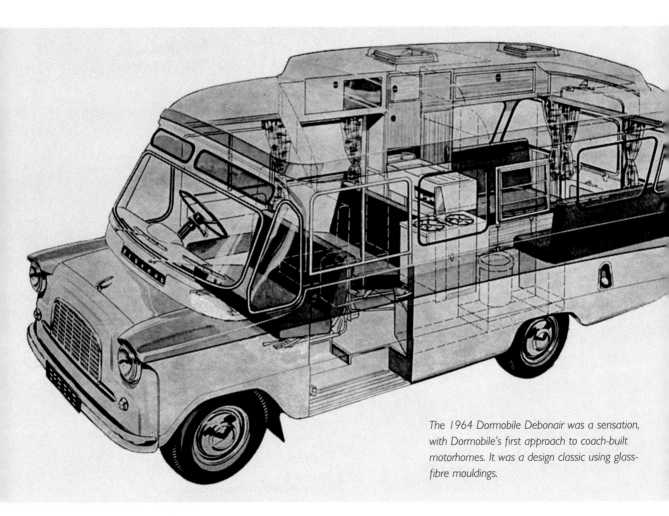

The 1964 Dormobile Debonair was a sensation, with Dormobile's first approach to coach-built motorhomes. It was a design classic using glass-fibre mouldings.

The Debonair could be upgraded with a fridge and different colours were available for the exterior waistband.

Building Debonairs wasn't an easy operation, with investment in special moulds and skilled staff needed, but they sold well.

Turner's, as Wilson's, stocked a vast choice of campervans and motorhomes from UK makers. Greens of Epping were another growing motorhome dealership, as was Madison's, another big multi-franchise set-up, at Southport and later near Blackpool.

The 1970s would see a boom and bust era in motorhome makers. Exports from the UK into Europe were healthy. CI Motorised, the motorhome side of the CI Touring Caravan Group, became Autohome and brought in some very good designs, including over-cab sleeping (although the idea was originally from the USA).

Motorhomes were generally getting better equipped, with electric water pumps from Whale replacing the old foot/hand-operated units. Fridges by Electrolux operated on three power sources and also became larger in capacity. Truma convector heaters made by Carver Engineering also became a must-have for those using their motorhomes in out-of-season times. Gas lights would be replaced by florescent 12-volt units and hot water would even allow showers in some washroom designs.

The Debonair laid the foundation stone for the later Landcruiser, which used a full glass-fibre body shell. These are production images.

London-based Turner's had become another large motorhome and
campervan dealership. They attended outdoor shows in the 1970s.

With motorhome ownership increasing, dealerships became larger.
This is Madison's Kirkham (Blackpool) branch in 1976. It's now the
much-enlarged sales ground of Preston Caravans and Motorhomes.

Opposite: *Hilton motorhomes were built on the Isle of Man in the 1970s by Spacemaker Group. The luxury VW LT-based Hilton was a niche seller.*

In the early 1970s more new makers of motorhomes appeared. One was luxury maker, Hilton, which was based on the new VW LT chassis. Built in the Isle of Man (part of the Spacemaker Group), it was superbly made and lavishly equipped with heating, hot water, fridge, mains electricity and a big price tag. But by mid-1977, Hilton had stopped production.

There were also more new chassis to build on, including Toyota's Hi Ace 1.6 petrol engine, which would be a choice for new maker, Newlander Caravans in Hull, and also Dormobile in 1973. Their New World coach-built was stylish (designed by Ogle Design – responsible for the Bond Bug, Raleigh Chopper and Reliant Scimitar), but its high sides and narrow wheelbase were prone to being blown around in strong winds. It was well equipped and cost a hefty £2,020, but it was dropped after a year.

Above: *The two-berth Hilton with a caravan layout was very highly specified, with heating and mains electrics.*

Below: *The Dormobile New World (launched in 1973), based on a Toyota 1.6 petrol base, was seen as another Debonair but it flopped because of its poor handling.*

Newlander, a new maker in Hull, also used the new Toyota base. The Newlanders had basic interior finish.

Memories: David Wilkinson, owner of A-Line Caravans – We used to do a hire fleet, and me and my wife would clean them out and get them ready for the next customers. We also sold them, of course, but those days were good, although hard work!

With Commer and the popular Ford Transit now real favourites for coach-built motorhomes, owners had plenty of choice. They were nearly all petrol engines, although some of the larger coach-builts from Jennings and Cotswolds used mainly Mercedes diesel units. Ken Stephens' Cotswolds were super-luxury models and at the Earls Court Caravan Show in 1969, Lord Snowdon and Princess Margaret were photographed admiring the Mercedes-based luxury motorhome. (Did they buy one? No.)

Lord Snowdon and Princess Margaret inspect a Luxury Cotswold Mercedes-based motorhome at the 1969 Caravan Show at Earls Court.

The number of makers coming into the market of coach-built motorhomes was expanding. Touring caravan bodies were now also being fitted onto a chassis cab, strange as it may seem. Some small concerns did this on demand for folk, while others were DIY conversions. Carlight luxury caravan builders built their caravans onto a Mercedes chassis – a novel idea that sold relatively well. One company named Apex also came up with this idea in 1972, using a then current Lynton five-berth caravan and mounting it on a Ford chassis with a V6 engine and a host of spec costing £3,000.

Carlight Caravans built Mercedes motorhomes with a Carlight caravan body attached.

Autosleeper of Oxley, Thomas Hodgkins of York, Richard Holdsworth, ICP and others were now having a slice of the motorhome market. The motorhome had become more affordable and retired couples found it ideal for continental travel. With the continent becoming more motorhome friendly, a holiday abroad was an easy option.

By the late 1960s, retired folk were looking at the advantages of buying a motorhome, travelling abroad to various countries (in many cases following the sun), then coming back to the UK for a further few months. Some retired owners rented out their houses which paid for their continental trips. The motorhome was very appealing. It was easy to just take off at a moment's notice and with the larger designs, it was very self-contained.

By the 1960s, motorhome owners were going abroad more often – a Bluebird Highwayman comes off the Hoverlloyd in 1968.

*The motorhome was being advertised as a perfect way to spend
your retirement in the late 1960s.*

Cherry Blossom

Nimes Arena

The Dolomites

Springtime
in England

Summer in France

Autumn in Italy

PLANNING RETIREMENT?
A LONG CAREFREE HOLIDAY?

Memories: Derek Andrews, owner of LeisureDrive Campervans – My dad had fancied the idea of a motorhome and duly he and I converted an old BMC ambulance, as often folk did! But we decided to make it a very practical design and it was sold within days in early 1969. We bought another, and me and my wife and daughter would spend weekends away enjoying the freedom. That was the foundation of my business, 50 years later!

Another form of the motorhome was the demountable design, which was a US idea. UK maker Suntrecker used Bedfords and Transits to attach the body to. It became quite successful in its niche market. It introduced more models and a few others joined in this marketplace but Suntrecker was to be the most successful. Island Plastics bought the idea but had limited success with small glass-fibre body shells.

In 1973, VAT was added to motorhomes and the oil crisis also played its part in knocking sales. Profits began to slide and makers went out of business. The big Hull caravan maker, A-Line, went into motorhome production, with its Advantura range based mainly on Bedford CFs. They sold well and had a good range of four-berth layouts. (When the Bedford CA was replaced by the CF, it was a far better chassis to build on and was a popular choice for many convertors and coachbuilders.)

Derek Andrews.

Once off the cab it was used like a caravan!

IPC were the makers of the new Suntrecker in 1973. This launched the demountable – a US idea. It was available on Ford and Bedford CF chassis cabs.

Above: *A-Line Caravans in Hull began building motorhomes from around 1977. This is a later model. After A-Line went bust, a new owner took the Advantura range on.*

Opposite: *By 1971, CIM became CI Autohomes. This new design, shown here at the factory, was easy to mount on all the popular new chassis brands.*

The end of the 1970s saw sales decline and even CI Autohomes was struggling after expanding its range and producing new designs and production methods. Its Parkstone factory exported to Europe, with the Autohome's easy to adapt coach-built body suitable for various chassis makers. The CI Autohome was one of the UK's best-selling motorhomes, with its style inside and out. Autohome produced some very good-looking, practical motorhomes in the 1970s.

Left: *The Autohome was stylish and very popular at home and for exports. It was well equipped and also came with family layouts. This one is a 1974 year.*

Right: *Autohome interiors were very 1970s, and practical too.*

Dormobile had been bought out by Coalite, while others such as Jennings bowed out. The next few decades would see big changes in the motorhome industry – new names would come to the fore, mainly from established caravan manufacturers such as Swift, Lunar, Elddis and Compass; some well-known names would go, and others would be taken over. Our next chapter will take us to the present day, with new imported brands coming in from Europe, there were definitely changes ahead!

Left: *Jennings luxury Roadrangers were popular for older motorhome users in the 1970s.*

4.
The 1980s' Motorhome Sales Boom to the Present

The end of the 1970s saw the motorhome industry hit hard by a general recession – and it wasn't just motorhome sales, touring caravans were also given a rough ride. Dealerships would see troubled times and some of the well-established names would close.

Dormobile, the name that even non-motorhome users knew, was starting to take a tumble. Their Deauville coach-built used bonded sides to replace the traditional bodywork but it received a lukewarm reception. Dormobile had got involved with touring caravan production in late 1969, aiming to take the touring market by storm, but it didn't happen. However, by late 1976 Dormobile had relaunched into tourers with some advanced designs. But by the early 1980s, Dormobile had gone, the factory flattened. Amazingly, no other manufacturer took the name on. Perhaps the stiffer competition had hit Dormobile as hard as the downturn.

CI Autohomes would also see its parent company collapse in 1982, but the Autohomes

Dormobile, by the early 1980s, were launching a new coach-built
– the Deauville – but sadly Dormobile went out of business.

side had launched a new Highwayman which had been well received. A management buyout set the company back up as Autohomes UK.

Large dealership group, Gailey, with its fifteen UK branches selling tourers as well as motorhomes, also hit the buffers, closing down all its branches. Godfrey Davis Group lost its battle and closed.

But companies did survive, and there were still buyers for new and used motorhomes. However, new sales were down, and it seemed the motorhome boom of the late 1960s and early 1970s was never to return. The motorhome, though, was finding favour with sportsmen and women for events. One such was John Davis, an England International Speedway star. In 1980, CI loaned him a CI Travelhome, giving it publicity in return.

Companies such as Autosleeper, with its successful coach-built from 1976, began developing new glass-fibre coach-built models and the mid to late 1980s saw some successful models with excellent quality interiors. As mentioned in the last chapter, in the early 1980s, Compass Caravans launched two coach-builts on Mercedes chassis cabs – Clipper and Drifter. Swift had built a prototype by late 1983–84, launching their first Kon-Tiki model in late 1985. Elddis also followed with its first Autostratus models in the same year and soon were building an A-class (where the motorhome's bodywork takes into the cab, these were popular abroad). Elddis, like Swift, would establish themselves quickly.

By 1983, the market was beginning to pick up slightly. This encouraged a few new makers and some importers. Hymer, the German manufacturer of high-class motorhomes, gained a slow but growing market share, Tabbert tried, but didn't do well with its A-class designs. Lunar Caravans at Preston, Lancashire, had also looked at motorhome manufacture and by 1984–85 they were producing two coach-built models on Mercedes 207 chassis cabs, although it wouldn't be until the early 1990s that they would gain more success with their popular Roadstar range.

Below: *The Autohome Highwayman was given a new look by the early 1980s, but the CI Group went into liquidation and its divisions were sold off.*

Opposite: *CI had loaned motorhomes out to various celebrities and sports persons such as speedway champ John Davies in the late 1970s.*

Autosleeper moved into motorhomes from campervans in 1976,
with their first smart-looking model on a Sherpa or Bedford.

Swift Caravans built their first motorhome prototype in early 1983, based on their Swift Cottingham tourer at the time.

Opposite: *Elddis Autostratus was the first take on a motorhome by the Elddis Caravan Company. By the early 1990s, they were well established in this area.*

Above: *Lunar, the lightweight caravan manufacturer, had built a prototype motorhome. By 1984–85 they were producing two layouts using Mercedes.*

Above: *Hymer had begun in 1957, but by the early 1980s they were getting well established in the UK as a premium German make.*

Opposite: *Tabbert would not be as successful in the motorhome market in the UK as Hymer, but they had some success with their caravans.*

E-CLASS MOTORHOMES

The most technically advanced and sophisticated leisure vehicles ever to appear on the British Market

Outright
winner
of the
National
Motor
Caravan
of the Year
Award
Germany
1981

Niche markets are always a risky side, but in 1983 a small maker set up, named Prince Motorhomes, from Bridport. What was unusual about their products was that you could have a car – yes, a car! – such as Ford Cortina MK3 or an Austin Maxi, converted to a coach-built motorhome. Today, safety approval would prevent these motorhomes being produced, but back then it wasn't an issue. They were compact, yes, but for some it was ideal. They were built mainly on Leyland cars, but I have seen a Cortina MK3 and a Volvo 144 with a Prince conversion. Sadly, few survive.

By the mid-1980s, although many of the older makers had gone, there were new ones popping up such as Auto Trail. Barry Holmes and Bill Boasman, who had both worked for Mustang Caravans, had now gone into repairing caravans and motorhomes. Designing their first coach-built on a Peugeot, by 1983–84 they were trading as Auto Trail Motorhomes, building mainly on Mercedes. They became more popular with the new interest in motorhomes and eventually

they were taken over by ABI Caravans, but would be sold to the French Trigano Group after ABI went into liquidation in 1997.

A small maker, Foster & Day, had limited success building on various chassis, although mainly Fords, while Apollo, not far from Rochdale-based Foster & Day, was to concentrate on demountables and custom-built motorhomes – again, another niche sector.

Imported makes were making ground, although slowly at first. The new Autohomes UK relaunched some new models and brought the Highwayman name back, along with a new model based on a Bedford Rascal mini pick-up in 1986. Named the Bambi and sleeping two people, this compact motorhome hit it right. Although it was a niche product, it sold well (for £7,919) and even had an owners' club!

Autosleeper had increased its coach-built range with its superb quality built furniture. They sold well and gave the brand another expanding market to add to their campervans. Names such as Talisman, Clubman and Legend were popular

Prince motorhomes would convert a family car into a motorhome in 1983, using mainly the Austin Maxi and Austin Ambassador.

Introducing the Prince Conversion

luxury coach-builts that can still be seen today in good numbers and still providing pleasure.

As motorhome ownership increased, the mid to late 1980s saw a boom in sales. Swift and Compass had expanded their motorhome ranges and production. The Talbot Express chassis were proving popular and there was a growing change to diesel engines, with the French leading the way. Fiat was fast catching up (Ducato) as preferred bases for coach-built motorhomes. Some dealers, such as Brownhills (who imported Hymers), grew, as did the Marquis Group, who had begun in 1973. Hampshire & Dorset Motorhomes opened a new showroom in the early 1980s, expanding its operation at a time when sales were still recovering from the start of the 1980s.

Opposite: *By 1989, Auto Trail had become a successful motorhome manufacturer with a good choice of layouts and a distinctive profile.*

Right: *The traditional interior of the Auto Trail Sioux family model from 1989.*

Above: *Small motorhome manufacturers such as Foster & Day, near Rochdale, built mainly to order on most chassis makes.*

Opposite: *After CI Autohomes, a new Autohomes UK was formed. One of their successful niche models was the micro Bambi motorhome in 1985.*

Opposite: : *By the early 1980s Autosleeper had redesigned and expanded their motorhome range with a quality build and well-finished interiors.*

Right: *The Bambi interior was compact but filled a gap in this market sector and even had an owners' club!*

Below: *Marquis, who had begun in 1973, also slowly began to expand its operations.*

Some motorhome dealers looked ahead. Hampshire & Dorset opened a new showroom in 1983.

With the bulk of motorhomes now having double glazing and blown-air heating, they could be used all year round, and parks were now becoming more motorhome friendly, supplying electrics, emptying and water points as well as more hard-standing pitches. The motorhome was a growing sector. There were several publications around that were dedicated to the motorhome buyer, such as *Three Ms* and *Motor Caravan Magazine*. Several books were written to help folk chose a motorhome, with information on where to go in them.

The 1980s may have begun in gloom but by 1989, the economy was on a high. Into the 1990s and the motorhome presence was growing in shows such as the Birmingham NEC Caravan & Boat Show. Autohomes UK would fall in 1992, when one of the main driving forces, Ian McPherson, died, but Elddis purchased the name. It renamed the Bambi (Nipper), but it never had the same success.

A new maker set up out of the old ashes of Autohomes UK, named Herald, which was then bought out by Compass, who were then purchased by Explorer Group Elddis! Compass had new names, such as Calypso and Navigator, join its Drifter range. Luxury caravan maker Buccaneer had begun making luxury motorhomes in the late 1990s. Explorer bought the company and then relaunched Buccaneer Motorhomes, but they were only around for a few seasons.

Compass had vastly increased their motorhome ranges by the mid-1990s, including the 1994 Navigator 360.

Imported motorhomes were arriving from the likes of Adria. They had a simple profile but were well made and offered a different interior to UK models. Pilote, the one-time French caravan manufacturer, changed production to motorhomes and tried to woo UK buyers. Ci, in Italy – not the UK Ci, but formed from that old company – was now producing good value-for-money motorhomes with family layouts. The spec wasn't great but they would prove to be a practical design. US Travelworld motorhomes had a small niche market in the UK, while more mainstream imports were Sun Roller, Home Car, Geist, Burstner and Dethleffs.

The number of imports would grow further by the start of the 2000s. There were still some smaller makes such as Eagle, Daytona and Nu Venture around but more and more imported makes were hitting the UK shores.

Navigator 360 interior was very traditional, and Compass appealed to older buyers.

Hobby Motorhomes came into the UK with some stylish coach-builts boasting strong build quality. Knaus, the German maker, also hit the UK, along with Weinsberg. Swift now had a strong portfolio which included several price points with its ranges such as Capri, Sundance and Kon-Tiki. Lunar had also extended its motorhome range and when the company was purchased by the Tirus Group, several motorhomes were imported with the Lunar badge attached. Lunar Champs and Chateaus were launched in the mid-2000s, by which time Lunar had also extended its Roadstar range to Telstar and Newstar, using mainly Fiat chassis but also Renaults.

Holdsworth was eventually dropped, becoming Cockburn–Holdsworth and became Autocruise by the mid-1990s. This was another quality coach-built range of motorhomes that would gain a good reputation over the years. Autocruise would also take over the 1970s Pioneer motorhome name. Auto Trail had grown, with new layout additions and their motorhomes were also easy to spot on the road with their profile. It's not uncommon to see late 1980s Auto Trail motorhomes still giving good service. Under Trigano, Auto Trail have one of the most up-to-date motorhome production plants in Europe with several ranges being built.

Adria Caravans began importing motorhomes in the mid-1980s with the Talbot-based Adriatik. By the 2000s, they had vastly increased their UK presence.

Nu Venture, based in Wigan, made coach-built compact
motorhomes, carving a niche market for themselves. This is the
Surf on a Citroen. (Photograph by Andrew Jenkinson)

From their early Kon-Tiki range, Swift soon expanded their motorhome line-ups with models like the strong-selling Sundance in 2005. (Photograph by Andrew Jenkinson)

Lunar were sold to the Tirus Group in the early 2000s and imported Lunar badge models such as the Champs. (Photograph by Andrew Jenkinson)

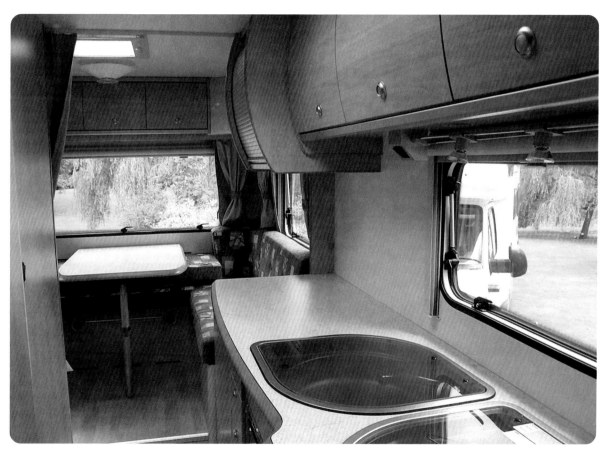

The Champ interior was typically continental in design but it didn't sell well. (Photograph by Andrew Jenkinson)

Valentine

Volkswagen based motor caravans by Richard Holdsworth

Left: *The 1994 Holdsworth Valentine would have a modern interior – the Valentine was based on the successful Ranger from previous years.*

Opposite: *The Compact Auto Trail Tracker FB 2018 model offered a well-equipped motorhome for those wanting a transverse fixed-bed layout in a narrower width. (Photograph by Andrew Jenkinson)*

The name Bessacarr, a mainly caravan brand bought by Swift in 1996, was used to give Swift another motorhome brand that gave a well-specified motorhome. In 2001 Swift purchased ABI UK tourer brands, including Ace. Being known for the caravan range, Swift decided to do a modern interior motorhome range, giving it the Ace name. The Ace motorhomes had family and also couples' layouts and gave Swift a slice of the market that the imported makers were taking. Aces ran for some years before being dropped as Swift reorganised its motorhome brands.

In the early start of the 1990s UK manufacturers started a trend with dealers taking a standard range of motorhomes then adding extras to it and renaming it as a dealer 'special'. Both Swift and Elddis tried this. Tying up with a dealer for 'specials' meant that the manufacturer had a firm order for batches. It wasn't long before most large dealerships took on this idea, adding extra kit for less than a customer buying a standard model.

Fixed beds have become the must-have layout for many. (Photograph by Andrew Jenkinson)

Swift used the Bessacarr Caravan name to make a range of upmarket motorhomes in the mid-1990s, from models accommodating couples to family ones. (Photograph by Andrew Jenkinson)

The 2008 Ace Roma by Swift, with fixed bed and overhead cab double bed – the Ace range was developed to compete with the increasing imports such as Elnagh, McLouis, CI Motorhomes and Roller Team. (Photograph by Andrew Jenkinson)

Marquis produce one of the most popular dealer 'specials' – the Majestic, based on the Elddis Autoquest range. (Photograph by Andrew Jenkinson)

Autocruise had, in the late 1990s and early 2000s, made a successful number of 'specials' for Marquis. Elddis became very good at doing this and its most well known for the Majestic, which was made for Marquis Group and is still a current model. From the 1990s Elddis grew its range, dropping the Autohomes name after a few years. The Elddis Sunseeker range launched for 2001, creating a more upmarket Elddis line-up than the successful Autoquest. The Compass brand became more regimented with the Elddis influence and made an identical range named the Avant-garde.

Marquis had also been involved with 'specials' from Autocruise, the South Yorkshire manufacturer who would eventually become part of Swift Group by 2006. Autocruise had built up a very good following, manufacturing several ranges, and names such as Stargazer, Vision and Valentine would become well known among motorhome owners. Out of the demise of the Autocruise name, after a few years in coach-builts with Swift basically just concentrating

Mains corner lighting and hardwood edges on lockers were all part of the Sunseeker specification, along with good storage.

on campervan designs for Autocruise, a new company named Bentley Motorhomes emerged. Bentley produced something that the Autocruise models would have looked like and they were selling quite well by 2011, but the company ran into problems and was then sold to luxury maker Vanmaster Caravans.

However, production never began. With only two prototypes being built Vanmaster went into liquidation. Imported makers were taking a firm hold in the UK, so it was breaking news in early 2002 that caravan manufacturer Avondale was to enter the motorhome sector. It used Fiat Ducato chassis and turbo diesels. All motorhomes now sold were the new models that had a leaning towards the Autosleeper coach-built range using glass-fibre body panels.

Marquis Group had expanded over the years, adding new dealerships. They also began their own 'specials' from Autocruise in 2000, which sold well.

The 2001 Sunseeker range from Elddis was upmarket, with a host of extras and upgraded interior furniture finish.

Bentley Motorhomes, in 2012, at the NEC Caravan Motorhome Show, were well-finished-off motorhomes. (Photograph by Andrew Jenkinson)

Left: *Interiors were well equipped, nicely finished and stylish too.*

Below left: *Avondale motorhomes showed plenty of promise from 2002, with good model choices – but a few years later, they were ended.*

Below right: *Avondale's range were good-looking motorhomes, but the company had stopped producing them by 2006.*

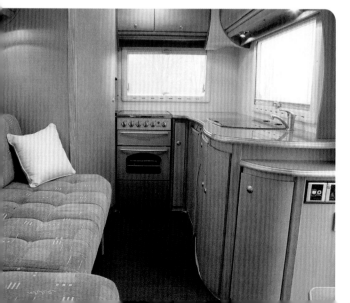

Two ranges were produced. They were Seascape and Seaspray, with various layouts and specifications. They were quite well received by the press and after a few teething faults they seemed set to establish themselves, with dealerships being set up. The move into the motorhome business cost the company a large investment, but unfortunately, after just a few years they dropped the motorhome ranges and this perhaps cost the company its survival. By late 2008, the Avondale caravan production was wound up.

Bailey Caravans of Bristol, who had seen a massive sales upturn in the late 2000s for their popular touring caravan ranges, were to also enter the motorhome market. They developed their own construction idea, naming it Alu-Tech, which would be ideal for their motorhome division. They had used it on their caravans from 2010. From late 2011, they launched their new Approach line-up based on a Peugeot chassis. The success of these saw the company expand its ranges. Some sold well, but others, such as their compact models (a narrower-width motorhome) didn't do as well.

Even so, Bailey have become a firmly established manufacturer of motorhomes in the UK, carving themselves out a slice of the motorhome market sector with their Autograph line-up.

Fun Fact: If you go out for the day in your motorhome, it's been known for another caravan or motorhome to have taken your place when you return – so, folks leave chairs and even signs saying, 'Stay off our pitch!'

By 2001, a new motorhome magazine would prove to become a popular read for motorhome owners. *Practical Motorhome* was originally launched by Haymarket Group then moved into new ownership with Future Publications and became a top-selling motorhome magazine.

With the 2010s, the motorhome was being seen as a leisure vehicle that retired folk were purchasing. Caravan parks were catering more for motorhomes, with new level pitches and even the Caravan Club spending vast amounts to

Bailey Caravans entered the motorhome market with value-for-money motorhomes named Approach. This is the Approach 740SE.

change its name to the Caravan & Motorhome Club to show that the club fully accepted the motorhome and the campervan. The freedom and now vast choice of motorhomes on the market, plus the shows and caravan dealers also selling motorhomes, meant the motorhome had truly come from being a niche idea to many taking up the hobby. Families were also coming more into motorhome ownership, discovering the ideal of just stopping off as and when you can.

The interior of the Bailey Autograph, from 2017, with twin fixed beds. (Photograph by Andrew Jenkinson)

The Caravan & Motorhome Club site at Sandringham shows how motorhomes are now catered for with more level pitches – 2014 Autosleeper Broadway. (Photograph by Andrew Jenkinson)

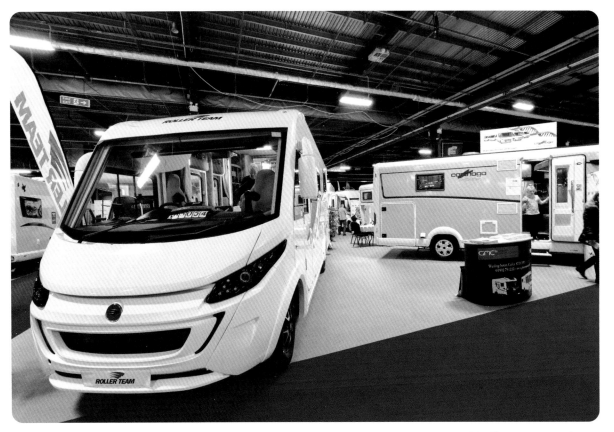

Shows such as those held at the NEC offer a great deal of choice for those buying a new motorhome. (Photograph by Andrew Jenkinson)

Above: *Over the years, the motorhome has become popular with younger families. (Photograph by Andrew Jenkinson)*

Opposite: *Some motorhome owners also tow a car behind for daily use if they are stopping at one place for several days. (Photograph by Andrew Jenkinson)*

Some motorhome owners began to take a small car to tow behind the motorhome, to give them more options if they were stopping in one location for several days. Many also began to take scooters and pedal cycles with special fixing brackets. Swift began adding the fixing points for carriers, and the rear large boot (known as a garage) has also become popular on motorhomes, especially the imported makes. The electric bike has also seen a rise in sales, mainly to motorhome owners as they are ideal to charge easily on site. At one time pre-1990s, few people used their motorhomes during the winter, but with blown-air systems and wet central heating, winter motorhome use has grown greatly over the last decade. This has also seen the motorhome hold even more appeal to users as they are now all-year-round leisure vehicles.

The electric bike has become a useful form of transport for motorhome users, with many motorhomes having a 'rear garage' to store them. (Photograph by Andrew Jenkinson)

More couples over the last few years have become motorhome owners, enjoying the comfort for touring at home and abroad. (Photograph by Andrew Jenkinson)

The modern motorhome is now also seen in in the winter months, with many used over
Christmas and the New Year period. (Photograph by Andrew Jenkinson)

Memories: Peter and Janet Washington, with their Dethleffs Global GT7 – Peter says, 'We love our Dethleffs motorhome. With its narrow width of 2.2m, it's easy to drive over narrow roads and through small villages. Ours has a fixed bed and excellent washroom, too, while a rear garage means we can get our electric bikes in out of the way. We love travelling to the Netherlands to our favourite site at Delft. It's so easy to cycle into the historic town centre.'

Recent years have seen more new layouts, with fixed beds, in particular, being popular. Adria, Swift and Elddis have launched several of these models over the last few years, catering for a niche in the motorhome market sector. Getting off the beaten track, exploring back roads and parking in small laybys for a stopover lunch is easier with a compact motorhome.

The modern motorhome has car-like driving and modern exterior styling, while interiors have left the more traditional designs of the mid and pre-2000s, making them far more appealing. Chausson, the French manufacturer under Trigano Group, as UK Autosleeper and Marquis Leisure Group, have come up with contemporary designs and they also use the latest Ford Transit – a name that has been around in motorhomes since 1965!

Swift continue to be the UK's biggest motorhome manufacturer, followed closely by Elddis, who became part of Hymer a couple of years ago. Hymer produce some extremely well-made and designed motorhomes along with Niesmann+Bishcoff. These are top luxury A-class models. In fact, Hymer has twenty brands of caravans and motorhomes, and recently Hymer were purchased by giant US Thor Industries, which are famous for their Airstream brand.

One thing is for sure, the design of the motorhome will no doubt change over the coming years, especially with electric being developed to power vans and lorries as well as cars. I just wonder what those motorhome users from the 1920s would say about the 'new marvels' of today?

Above: *Peter and Janet Washington's Dethleffs motorhome on site in the Netherlands.*

Opposite: *A compact motorhome, such as the Swift Rio shown here, is ideal for getting more off the beaten track or having a single-night stopover. (Photograph by Andrew Jenkinson)*

Above: *This Chausson Flash kitchen is fitted with small oven/ grill. Note the continental-style, modern interior. (Photograph by Andrew Jenkinson)*

Opposite: *Imported makes such as the French Chausson Flash have been using the Ford Transit base. (Photograph by Andrew Jenkinson)*

The 2019 revamped Swift Kon-tiki is a luxury six-wheel motorhome,
ideal for long European tours. (Photograph by Andrew Jenkinson)

The interior of the luxury Kon-Tiki with large lounge area.
(Photograph by Andrew Jenkinson)

100 years separate these two motorhomes!

Back then, motorhomes were the height of advanced design, but the same principle applies today in 2021 as it did a century ago, and that was the road to freedom and being able to take off at a moment's notice and discover new places making memories. The motorhome story is an interesting one and today it should be remembered – and I hope I have been able to show the roots of this pastime. Those early motorhome users/pioneers often risked life and limb, discovering new vistas and often travelling dangerous routes across deserts. Luckily for us, they recorded the tales in words and even pictures.

I hope you have enjoyed this story of the motorhome, over a century of development.

The modern motorhome has over 100 years of heritage and it provides adventures and memories today, just as it did back in the early 1900s.